ABOUT THE AUTHOR

Leon Priestnall was a poet based in Birmingham. He performed his poems up and down the country, headlining at The Door in the Birmingham Rep and performing spontaneous verse on BBC Radio. He was also host and founder of Birmingham spoken word night Howl. This was his first and only collection of poetry and is a retrospective of his work between 2007 and 2017. Leon passed in January 2021.

https://vervepoetrypress.com/2018/05/10/leon-priestnall/

www.facebook.com/leonpoetry

Leon Priestnall
Bennetts Hill Blues

VERVE
POETRY PRESS
BIRMINGHAM

PUBLISHED BY VERVE POETRY PRESS
Birmingham, West Midlands, UK
www.vervepoetrypress.com
mail@vervepoetrypress.com

FIRST PUBLISHED JUNE 2018
REPRINTED JAN 2019

Printed and bound in the UK
by Imprint Digital, Exeter

ISBN: 978-1-912565-04-7

*For my Mother
and in loving memory
of my Father.*

CONTENTS

Bennetts Hill Blues

The Sun On The Hill

Half drunken slobs
and filled-with-self-pity fights.
Wine bottle wisdom
guides us through these city nights.

The pretty types, wild with the *bad boys*
as *nice guys,* wallow in their beer.
An old eccentric on his own,
holding the bar, observes the madness through his sneer.

A single woman in her fifties,
but no more than twenty in her mind
shakes in bullet dodging fashion
as if for her tonight's designed.

A young man of twenty four is sober
preparing for his next fight.
A boxer, with a release for his aggression -
the calmest one around us, the most chilled out one in sight.

A former womaniser broods
because he's finally broken hearted.
Broke his rule and fell in love,
now he's back where he started.

And a married man grabs a bloke by the collar
just for flirting with his misses.
It calms down after five minutes,
then it's back to hugs and kisses.

A pseudo intellectual rambles philosophy,
he's Aristotle with a bottle,
babbles louder than the music,
stream of consciousness full throttle.

And the indie lads are quite keen
in their tight jeans
hoping to find fiends
to fulfill their hipster dreams.

As a drag queen takes a drag of a cigarette,
a mad crack addict
with a passion for ballet
stops in front of them and pirouettes.

A group of wannabe thugs in the corner,
they nod their head to the beat.
All of them went to private school
but they want you to think they're street.

And whilst all this is going on
the Poet just sits and feeds,
digesting from the narratives
to fulfill artistic needs,

to tell stories of betrayal,
of ecstasy and bliss,
that hard knock punch
the sweetest kiss.

Stories heavenly, stories foul,
they howl them!
so you know that the flow is strong.

So sit back and listen
as the Poet
let's you know what is going on.

Collision

Charming folk with style's fine,
but throwing up that vile wine?

Unrivalled angst.
Give me something to whine about and I'll pine

without a doubt.
I haven't got a clue.
I'm caught somewhere
between her mean curves and her tattoo.

I'll take two shots for the needy in me,
two more to lower my inhibition.
Too much it's all rather queasy in me
and pick a bathroom stall for intermission.

The fact they're on a date with me
makes me doubt their intuition.
Two heads are better than one
unless it increases indecision.

Johnny

He walks through the deep night
married to the street lights
and the ladies say they like him,
in his stories they delight.

He's a beautiful loser,
a frustrated odd villain.
He likes Leonard Cohen,
Tom Waits and Bob Dylan.

He thinks current pop culture is getting stale.
In love with the underdog,
he says fuck off to the daily mail.

He finds all attention flattering.
Like a tease he works the club's with ease
and watches rejection sting.

He's a flat out scoundrel rat
with a scowl, prowling round your council flats.

Alarmingly charming,
he'll fratanise and mutter
street poetry that'll romanticise the gutter.

He stands tall
in the whirlwind at the world's end,
his hand through his hair,
his eyes on your girlfriend!

He's a sees-clear-through-his-squint dishevelled whino
who finds hope in the neon lights of spearmint rhino.

So cool,
he finishes a cigarette with one drag.
Never votes Tory
and thinks they're all scumbags.

With deep blue sea eyes
that with one look could cure disease
but deep down
he's a tortured ball of insecurities.

No, no man honestly could say
that they
wouldn't wannabe Johnny for the day.
The way he dresses,
impresses,
and eases those stresses with grace,
so why
do I
want to punch Johnny in the face?

Is it because I see through his nonsense
and can tell he's a spiteful crook?
or is it because I'm envious of his movie idol looks?

The way he seduces the girls
and leaves me in the corner some dumb clown
basking in the shadows
of this Brando of Brum town.

Or is that lovable charm?
That charm which disarms
and can be quite sinister,
poisoning the well from which it draws
like charm in a prime minister
can lead to illegal wars,

or is it because

when he stood tall
in the whirlwind at the world's end
his hand through his hair
his gaze was on MY girlfriend!

And everybody forgives him like
oh Johnny, you rascal
oh Johnny, you rascal
oh Johnny, you arsehole!

I can't forgive your charm
and I can't forgive your grace,
and Johnny, yes Johnny
I want to punch you in the face.

But honestly,
frustratingly,
there is no way I can say
that I wouldn't want to be Johnny for the day.

Bothersome Beauty

Does it bother you,
that I find your beauty so bothersome,
that it stays with me throughout each week?

Whether greeting or paroozing
eating or up late from lack of snoozing,
thoughts of you abound without you around.

Whether working or trying to pay bills,
I lack the keep-your-beauty-at-bay skills.

The sight of you thrills
but the plight of you kills.

I'm not sure what's polite to do?
Say *hi* to you
or slightly seduce another girl on your view
and pretend to be aloof?
I'd probably fail.
The other girl would bail
and on a glass of wine I'd chip my tooth.

Your beauty lies
in that smile
and that mind behind your eyes.
Your beauty never lulls.
It puts the lust in heavy metal
and the softness in lullabies.
It both strengthens and yet burdens our ties.

So how can I pretend and get on with my day
when I know that such beauty exists?
How can I pretend you remain undiscovered
when the pain of your beauty persists?

I'm sorry, I'm sorry,
I'm sorry, I'm sorry,
sincerely I apologise if you're pissed.

If it bothers you
that I find your beauty so bothersome.

Painted Jar

How far can I pursue the memory of a painted jar?

Strange music plays
through those art studio days.

I miss you.

I miss the dedication
in your focused eyes
as each brushstroke,
then,
creates something new for me to long for,
now.

Terrible

I'm a terrible smoker.
Not that smoking's terrible.
Just
I'm terrible at it.

Clumsily flicking lighters.
Fighting the wind to ignite.

It does.
A sense of triumph.

Easy Judgement

We see it. Abuse hurled in the form of judgement,
pleasure taken in another's embarrassment.

Fuck it! They deserve it. They knew what they were in for.

As the night falls the mood seems to fit easier,
running away from the mob, lost in the darkness.

Lost in darkness, running away. The only light,
the light from a torch a villager is weilding.

Taxi Girl

I watch
as she gets into the taxi.

She looks back.

I let the look linger
- a few glasses of wine
and a couple of awkward moments down the line -
a little bit too long.

She tells the driver the address of her flat,
a flat which is filled with unpacked suitcases.

And then she shakes her head.

And I watch as she shakes her head.

And all I'm thinking is,
I can't be that to you, Taxi Girl.

A couple of nights ago,
I was in the same bar
talking to a woman
who was anything other than herself.
She was presenting a peer pressure informed image
of what she presumed my so called *masculinity* wanted
        her to be.

And I carried on conversing,
carrying the same wallet
stuffed
with insecurities,
only buying drinks
with petty chit chat,
hoping she wouldn't ask me to reach into that wallet
to pay for anything.

And we went home together.
But I can't be that, to you, Taxi Girl

Yesterday,
somebody said,

Leon, you're a bastard who doesn't act like a bastard.
You're a needy insecure twat.
You seek my attention for you're own selfish validation.
Quote Sylvia Plath to acheive your Henry Miller ambitions.
And you can fuck right off, mate.

And I denied it,
but they were right.
But I won't be that to you, Taxi Girl.
No, I'll get it right this time.

If I'm ever that to you
it won't be with a guy
who let rejection teach him everything
and love teach him nothing.

It won't be with a guy
still living in a world
where people treat windows like mirrors
checking the reflection
to make sure their hair
is the right side of
just got out of bed with a stranger this morning.

If I'm ever that to you
it won't be some stupid one night stand
because you're lonely
and I'm available.

Because you're more than that.
You're like a preacher who doesn't even preach
but taught me the truth
with your eyes
reconfirming my faith in religion.

You're a rock 'n' roll Marilyn Monroe.
A ready to stay up until 3 am in the morning
talking about waiting for a sunrise
myth busting insomniac.

You're a truth telling jester,

a wisdom infused yarn spinner,

a soft landing sucker punch,
and you deserve better than that.

So let's stop with the cutting small talk,
agree to look after ourselves,
and then maybe,
m a y b e
we can be something for each other.

Sudden Ache

The canal, beautifully lit this spring night.
The high rise apartments head butting the sky.
And the cigarette that dangles from my lips
provides a mask of cool, hiding my envy.

Envy for the lovers and the groups of friends,
you know, the sort nights like tonight are built for.

And I start to think not just about her,
but the many *hers* I've thought about,

and then...

                there's an ache.

The Path

A dog dances on the edge of a canal boat.
How happily he occupies his time, so blissful.

I walk along, inhale the day's first cigarette.
Displeased with myself, I reflect on last night's sins.

I step aside as a cyclist rides on by.
I flick my finished fag to the cracked, cobbled path.

Lost in my mind, a battle of thoughts,
still reflecting on the previous evening.

The ducks leap out of the canal, scrambling for bread.
One duck lays down, tucks head away, seems quite content.

I carry on meandering along the path,
thinking back on the *who* I spent last night with.

Blockade

The sun shines down on this haven of innocence,
the chalk for the hop scotch practically glistening,

yet, nerves are crippling my eight year old body.
At least that's how it seems. They hide in the bushes.

I step forward. They appear and form a straight line.
They've made their blockade and there's nothing I can do.

Tactical and precise in their measures. So young,
still they know how to keep me out. A joke, to them.

Today, I decide to risk it. To run for it.
To enter what is by rights as much mine as theirs.

As I'm taken to the ground, arms around my throat,
my face hits the sun, still making the chalk glisten.

The Tree Stump of Solitude

In the corner of the playground was a tree stump,
and here little me sat in quiet observation.

Football conquered most, others enticed by kiss chase.
Of course in autumn conkers conquered all of us.

Loner was a nick name as given to me
by my peers as the situation that provoked it.

I sat quietly observing on my tree stump,
practising anger and not a part of anything.

Educated

We stood out in the hall, my friend and I,
looking at our shoes as school boys will do.

YOU TWO ARE A JOKE. ONE THAT'S NOT FUNNY,
the teacher screamed, no self control at all.

I looked up and caught my friend smirking away
as the teacher adds to our education.

A Kid

There they were, all the contents of my bag
emptied, spilling out over the toilet
seat, exercise books, toys and other things.

Teacher would eventually find out.
Obviously nothing would be done.
Playtime would come and I'd sit by myself.

I learnt what I would later read about
in the books of John Stuart Mill. I did.
Truth is, sometimes it's hard being a kid.

Barstool Blues

Barstool blues.
Haven't a penny symphonies.
Ego raves ear piercing electronica.
Wisdom finds it's way through a trusty harmonica.
Bartender pulls a red stripe.
Old man sips his pint.
Chef enjoys a tea.
Late shift ease
through minds eye wandering
just the right side of
I really shouldn't.
Couples out of the moment
but knee deep in it.
Camera phone
snap shot
projecting on to each other.
I want to get away from myself.
Serenades
why don't you love me?
Punch ups.
Competitive
compliments.

The Deep Down Whatever It Is

The deep down whatever it is.
Whatever it is, it's deep down.
The deep down whatever it is.

Celebrity is the new aristocracy.
It's a damn hypocrisy
and we misunderstand the plot.
Me, I'm just you're average swat,
alan watts, krishnamurti.
In this relationship we don't stand we squat
and, with love, I'm begging for you to hurt me.

I don't know what I'm doing.
We're toying with poison,
ashamed of ourselves
for how much we enjoy sin.
I wasted my entire youth on *clever*.
Now we waste our time
looking though each others phones searching for proof-
whatever,
together,
laughing at tv idiots but envious of their news feeds.
No news feeds us. Who treats each other well anyways?
You need me.

So busy, trying not to try. In the pursuit of non pursuing,
oblivious to the wrong we're doing.
Why don't we just be?
Why don't I regurgitate
ideas I didn't think of? Standing here, such a nervous state,
I find it hard to stand up straight.

Am I speaking correctly?
If not, please don't correct me.

I've watched music videos turn to pornography
quicker than politics turns to arguments
or a handshake can turn to a fist fight.
If I'm honest, I don't really give a shit
as long as I can ignore it
and the lighting is just right.

I've seen some turn their ideas
into their identity
and cling to it for years.

I've seen others use kindness,

nothing but love hypocrites.
Shirt and tie. Ha ha.
I-know-what-I-mean jibberish,
and I'm certain I'm ga ga.

Trying to attain something I already have
yet totally unaware I'm doing it when I do.
You are what you pretend to be.
A total idiot said that, but it's true.
Trying to find a view point.
Not a lot showing
to be comfortable in the not knowing....

It's similar to a kiss,
like the ones we share
and I don't ever want to miss.

The deep down whatever it is,
whatever it is, it's deep down.
The deep down whatever it is.

Amy

Amy is eating disorder skinny.

She just turned twenty five 'cos it's her birthday

and she's sitting at the bar getting drunk
whilst some half decent band
plays Bob Marley's *Is This Love* in the background.

And the boyfriend she met a couple of weeks ago
whom she's fallen head over heals for
but doesn't realise is only with her on a rebound
hasn't text her back all day.

And her best mate is trying to reassure her

It doesn't matter, it's his loss.
It doesn't matter, it's his loss.

but Amy doesn't care
and Amy is going to stress about it.

Because the woman who raised her
doesn't love her.
And the only one who listens
is her counselor.
And the only man who treated her right
is gay.
And all of her tattoos mean something
but nobody notices that.

And she's probably going to spend her birthday
getting drunk out of her skull

only to wake up the following morning
next to some pricky pick up artist
who knew how to seduce his way
into her low self esteem ex reinforced mind.

And her boyfriend never text her back.

Like Lightening

And from my work came a brief distraction.

It's funny that you're a brunette
because right then you're hair was like fire
and your skin like lightening and your eyes,
looking through us, created burnholes

and everything else seemed rather pale in comparison.

Riddled

Riddled with ticks and routines.
Yes, such odd behaviour.
Loss of confidence in
ones own body and soul.
Thoughts invading ones mind -
a harsh imprisonment.

Nothing is as simple as
closing a door, walking

up and down stairs. Oh no.
Observe your completely

ridiculous actions

and collapse into laughter.

Side By Side

The trouble is, these thoughts don't come and go.
They aren't visitors here for the weekend

but are a permanent member of the household
whose ongoing habits make one grumpy.

And there seems no way to show them the door.
A constant struggle to live side by side.

Loose Leaf

Your voice had the urgency
of a dear one calling.
Let it out, come what may,
like a loose leaf falling.

Simple And Plain

Whilst others are taking flight
and not returning home.
I'm torn between writing a treatise of great philosophical
    insight
or a cliché break up poem.

Whilst others are breaking the mold,
taking hold of art
and redesigning it in their name,
I'm simple and plain -
still startled by a song lyric that mentions rain.

As the political order collapses
beneath the narcissistic weight
of a post modern baby Hitler with a twitter -
the world ending
not with a bang or a whimper
but with a hipsters ironic wink -
I just sit and think
about how I have too much time to sit and think.

Jealousies, ambitions, decisions, indecision,
hits and misses, misses the point.

Aching joints, broken hearts,
taking the piss, art,
kisses, is's and ought's.
I find a momentary spark,
upon giving up the pursuit
of finding the reality behind my thoughts.

I was looking but couldn't find it.
I'm incredibly simple minded
and seemingly out to self destruct,
allowing myself to be bothered
by the actions of personas
we knowingly or unknowingly construct.

I wish I was unhurried, mild
unafraid, perhaps colder, not so wild.
Instead I'm thirty years old and still a bullied child.

Speaking philosophical wisdom
as I watch the codeine fizzle
but I like that I'm still startled
by a song lyric that mentions drizzle.

Should I write an essay of momentary importance
as if there's nothing else to do?
Or should we discover whether *I*
is just another name for *you?*

How Easy

You sit with your head rested against
the refreshingly cool window.

As your current mode of transport
zooms along, you try to catch the sights.

One can't help but notice how
easily

it all passes by...

Byron And Keats

(After *Taxi Girl*)

I don't know her friend
well enough to call him kind.
He's definitely accepting.
Well, he's sitting here with me, isn't he?

And he drinks his pint
at a good pace
as if he's well versed in using alcohol to relax.
Where as I'm drinking my pints
like they're pints of Pepsi
and the way this evening's going
they probably should be...

I wish I was in tune with the tunes playing.

It sounds like my kind of music.

But my friend, she left the table.

Left me sitting. With him.

And I'm amusing myself
with the most immaterial of musings.

Lately
I've been fixated
on the sort-of-rivalry between Byron and Keats.
No, really I have. I know!

And I imagine it holds some significance to my own
artistic struggles when really – I'm just struggling.

And my friend just left the table.
and I'm sitting with him...

What do we make of it?
What does he make of me?
What are we made of?
We don't make eye contact really.
We don't make ourselves the best we can be.
We don't make something of use.
We don't make the most of it.
We make ... small talk.

And I'm getting drunker.
And my friend -
she returns to the table, with a shot -
and right now I might not refuse a shooting.

This past week
I've been such a bag of nuroscies
that the slightest off hand comment
leaves me on the edge of Keatsean tears
that I try to disguise behind some Byronic witty barb
and then slap myself for being a wanker.

I go out,
in search of the all that can come from nothing.
I flirt as if I just invented the concept.
I take compliments like they're drugs.

And the best part about sex
is not so much what occurs on the sheets we lay on
but that it allows our minds to become a blank canvas.
plus, we're all flattered by those who don't mind our canvas
        of scars.

As a teenager,
my longings used to come out in shyness.
They still do when it matters
but not when it doesn't,
so I appear like I'm really enjoying myself
when nothing matters.

Now my friend -
she's entertaining the table with ease.
And I
just stare at the table
for a moment,
then run -
literally run -
from the table
and out the building.

A few nights back.
I sat out side a pub.
talking to a woman
who, in my flirtation,
had the nerve to call me a 'bullshitter'.
It bothered me.
for a whole week.

I wanted to respond,
'Fuck you I'm a bullshitter.
People develop protections, you know.
There is a thin line
between paranoia and insecurity.
And the worst of us
always seems to get the best of us.'
But I didn't say that,
because she was actually really nice.
and pretty.
And not pretty like a pop song
but pretty like a coming of age story
and she was pretty smart too
and I really want to get to know her...

And my friend -
she chases after me.
She wants me to come back.
And I apologise for my lack of social
niceties during the evening.
And she says

'Remember the story I told you last night.
I love it because it is me.
The noises we make
are all people can work with
when they have no comprehension
of what's inside.
Don't apologise for that.'

And I want to say thank you.
Thank you for being beautiful
in a way I'm still trying to capture in verse.

And for holding on to goodness
through choice and not through obligation.
For giving me confidence.
For not just taking the night but owning it
with full force
like some sort of free spirited
goodwill, self-help entrepreneur.

I want to say this to her,
but I don't.
I do say thank you.
And in my drunken state
continue to fixate
on the sort-of-rivalry between Byron and Keats,
not quite sure where I stand
but knowing that really
they stood for the same thing.

Sylvia

I'm sitting down
waiting for the play to begin.
I feel awkward
because everyone in the audience
has either come as a couple or a group of friends.

I am the only one here alone.

The play is being produced
by a small collective of actors and writers.
So it's not taking place in the main auditorium
but in the studio room next to it.

Which makes me feel more awkward
because when I look around
I can see everyone in the audience clearly.

I look in each persons face.
They're all so happy,
laughing and joking with their loved ones.
Why does it seem like everyone knows each other?
I feel like a stranger
whose gate crashed a reunion for old friends.

The lights dim down.

Total silence.

The play's starting.

Lights illuminate the stage.

Two actors.

Sylvia is the wife of Lee.

The play starts,
both of them standing on either side of the stage
analysing their relationship in a very Annie Hall-esqe way.
The play shows every part of their relationship.
How they met,
their first time,
and all their various separations.

As each scene unfolds
I'm becoming more and more involved with it.
And I'm so besotted with Sylvia.
I think I'm actually falling in love with her.
But I'm not envious of Lee.
I'm relating to him.
I'm becoming him.
This is MY relationship.
It's me who's kissing Sylvia.
It's me who's arguing with her.
It's me who's crying
because I didn't really want a trial separation.
And these are my tears of joy -
so happy that we've decided to give it another go.

This is the most intense relationship I've ever had.
Me and Sylvia decide that we're soul mates
in the happiest of endings.

I love you Sylvia.

The lights dim down.

I'm starting to feel reality creep in.

When the lights come back on
my dreams have been shattered
and my heart is damaged
beyond repair.

The actors take their bow.

Every member of the audience is on their feet except me.
I'm still unable to move.

I look around.
The smiles on people's faces are making me feel
     awkward again.

We all leave the studio.

I watch everybody walk off into the night.

Groups of friends laughing and joking.

Couples holding each other in their arms,
gazing into each others eyes
with a united wisdom,
like they've discovered how the world works or something.

I get into a taxi.

Remain silent the entire ride home.

Arrive to an empty house.

My note pad is still on the table.

A challenge.

And all of my love poems are not enough.

Worn Out

Outside of the rather uninviting city cafe
a tired-out lady stands smoking a cigarette on her break.

An overall adorned with the café's worn out slogan
loosely fits over her average-sized worn-down body,

as she puffs away with glee on her one joy of the day,
carefully inhaling, making sure not to waste it.

Through the cafe window you can see a TV set
hanging, rather noticeably, from the cafe walls.

Our prime minister is giving a tough, and yet trite, speech -
well, so the text says - their voice unheard on the muted set.

The lady takes in the last few puffs of her cigarette
savouring every last moment.

Then flicks it to the ground and stubs it out, completely.
And then walks back into the cafe to finish her shift.

Too Much

Sink, softly, in your seat.
There's nothing like that third glass of wine.

You ponder all the throwaway phrases repeated
     throughout the evening.

But you know, yes, you know,
that a sea of wine
and only that
will provide, the much referred to, plenty of fish.

There's plenty of smiles though,
all around,
except across your face, just a frown,
amongst these drunken revellers
lost in their self induced merriment.

Both pissed and pissed off in her absence.
Thing about the thing is
you never learnt
how not to unburden
your achy breaky
acoustically tuned ready-for-radio tortured lost soul.
Too trite. Too 'in....'

Still, alcohol hasn't seemed to kill all hope.
The hope she might appear through those doors
with her smile and her dismay.

The Game

Please don't play with my heart, my love.
Please cease this run of your cruel game.
Like all entertainment for sport,
it's fun, but pointless is the aim.

To hear cruel jokes from your sweet lips,
may make me want those lips much more.
So please, please don't pay lip service
to love, if it's more mine than yours.

Each time your look returns my looks
I'm not sure what I'm looking through.
And my heart, it quite simply aches
as you let this cruel game ensue.

Is it flattery you're after?
It's flattery you're seeking, right?
Should I flatter you my cruel one
in this unflattering light?

As pointless as your game may be
the point of my request is plain.
I'm addicted to your cruelty.
It's a request I've made in vain.

Poem

It's funny, how her name falls from your lips.
Not out of love but out of how easily it does.

And that fire, that lights behind her mind, when said,
is a fire that keeps you both warm in different ways.

A flame lit, brightly provides some warming.
Yet, with a courage that can leave you quite startled

she will put out a candle with her fingertips.
This, however, is a flame that neither wants put out.

Know Her

know her
and know
the most
exquisite
distraction
from
the futility
of existence
ever known
by anyone
those all catching eyes
amongst
all that
dye splattered hair
to know
a regular
afternoon
from work
become
a haven to impulse
lost in her scent
every inch alive
lost
lost in her hair
lost
in the contemplation
of her cheek
her forehead

lost
lost
lost
lost
and
embarking further
until
we're both lost some more
buzzed
off
the irrelevance
of all else
but each other
and
our thoughts
her smile like a secret
we're getting further lost still
exhilarated
and ultimately
wanting
to get lost forever.

Leon Introduces...

Jack Crowe

When I first came across Jack Crowe he was participating in a local poetry slam. He was incredibly nervous, his note pad shaking in his hand. However, he stood out to me immediately. There was a charm in his nervousness and all the shyness in the world couldn't hide the biting wit of his verse. He has gone on to headline various spoken word nights and even put on one himself. Poem after poem he never ceases to impress me, each verse cleverly crafted without feeling forced and a sense of the absurd to put him up there with the best. Jack's poems inspire me to be a better poet, and I can't ask for more than that. So, here ya' go - Jack Crowe, one of my favourite poets.

Do You Wish To Continue?

At the checkout she stares with dead eyes
as her hands pass what shoppers want.
beep beep   *beep beep*

What creator would not be troubled,
would not press the mind, to find a solution
for this human, reduced to machine?

So it was that circuits were programmed,
by which we could serve ourselves.
She was made free.

In the gutter she stares with dead eyes
as shoppers pass her wanting hands.
spare change?   *spare change?*

What creator would not be troubled,
would not press the mind, to find a solution
for this human, reduced to machine?

Leon Introduces...

Bethany Slinn

Bethany Slinn is a powerhouse of the Birmingham arts scene. From organising events, political activism and work in the name of various causes she believes in, Bethany inspires through sheer force of will, charm, talent and, most of all, ethics and principles. However, the thing that first made me enchanted by Bethany was the power of her words. She is genuinely one of most talented poets out there, her poems are clever and vulnerable, and it's an honour to share some of her work with you.

When Something With A Purpose Doesn't Perform Its Basic Function

A blue biro that stops leaving ink on the page.

A bicycle with parallelogram wheels.

A chewing gum which fuses your jaw together.

A fidget spinner weighing 10 kg.

A perfume infusing the pheromones of your grandma.

An iphone which can access a menstrual cycle app to predict when you'll next ovulate, but can't accept a phone call.

A massage in which your masseuse asks you when you are planning on having children and prompts you to analyse your life plans, your ticking body clock and your entire existence.

A neurotransmitter which doesn't release enough serotonin.

A flat smile.

A friend who can't make you laugh.

A sister who doesn't give support.

A performer who can't stand on a stage.

A citizen who doesn't go outside.

A Selective Serotonin Re-uptake Inhibitor dose not taken because mind medicine is weak.

A rational judgement which impairs your health.

A realisation not acknowledged.

Leon Introduces...
Scarlett Ward

Scarlett is the poet I've been most recently introduced to of my three guest poets. I kept hearing her name everywhere. Have you read Scarlett Ward? Hey Leon, what do you think of Scarlett Ward's stuff? You know you'd love Scarlett Ward's poetry! To be honest, there was so much hype I became rather sceptical. Eventually I got to find out for myself. We were both published in the same anthology - Wild Dreams & Louder Voices - and to top it off our poems were published side by side. And I fell head over heels for her poetry straight away. So much so I'm featuring one of her poems in this very collection.
Lyrical, romantic and yet always clear and precise, Scarlett's poems are beautiful . Check it out for yourself.

Soft Palate

Memories of you force their way through.
Molars through the soft palate;
gristle of bone through
torn ligaments.

I try to knock the remaining ones out myself
with brick and rock
and rage.
My bloodied gums are relieved of you,
but I'm yet to clot.

When you hold it up to the light
missing you is just counterfeit loneliness.
Really, it's just an overflowing of empty,
as though you turned on the tap and walked away
and left me to mop up all that
nothing.

But I would rather spend these days alone
trying to contain all my grief in cupped hands
than pull the plug and have it all drain away.
Because it is a privilege to stand here
drenched in your consequence.

So now when we talk
our *hellos* are shaped like *I miss you*
and *goodbyes* are shaped like *don't leave*

again.
And the words bob around in the air between our mouths
like wilting balloons, with just enough jubilation left
in their sad foil corpses
that it's a shame to throw them away just yet.

ACKNOWLEDGEMENTS

Dad – I miss you everyday. I wish you were here to read this book. You were the most wonderful man I ever knew. In a way you are still here, in me. Thank you for everything.

Mum – You are my best friend. I'm sorry I let you down sometimes. We have each other. I love you.

Gerald and Claude – It's funny that you don't know each other and I felt the need to thank you together. You are the closest thing I have to brothers. Friends for life.

Stuart Bartholomew and Verve Poetry Press – Thank you for this opportunity and for taking a chance on me and this book. I can't wait for the magic Verve is going to continue to bring to the poetry world!

Jasmine Gardosi – You are the most original writer I've ever met. You inspire me, not just in art, but in life. You will change the world. It's an honor to call you my friend.

Mia – Thank you for everything.

Poetry jam/beatfreeks, Hit the Ode/Apples and Snakes, Grizzly Pear/Writers bloc, Stirchley Speaks and the entire Birmingham Poetry community. You are my home.

Joseph French – Thanks for asking me to put on a poetry night. Without you there is no Howl. This taught me more about myself than anything I've done. Thank you.

Bethany slinn, Jess Davies and Sean Colletti – You are beautiful humans and beautiful writers. Thank you for your help this past year.

Jerome – Thank you for putting up with my ego driven barstool rants for several years. You deserve more than a few medals. Thank you.

Jack Crowe and Scarlet Ward – Beautiful poem's each. Wonderful humans.

Taxi Girl – Thank you.

ABOUT VERVE POETRY PRESS

Verve Poetry Press is a new press focussing initially on meeting a local need in Birmingham - a need for the vibrant poetry scene here in Brum to find a way to present itself to the poetry world via publication. Co-founded by Stuart Bartholomew and Amerah Saleh, it will be publishing poets this year from all corners of the city - poets that represent the city's varied and energetic qualities and will communicate its many poetic stories.

As well as this wonderful collection from Leon - look out in 2018 for stunning first collections from Amerah, Casey Bailey Nafeesa Hamid, Rupinder Kaur, Kamil Mahmood and Hannah Swings, to name but a few. And watch this new press bring the colour and attitude of Verve Poetry Festival, our sister in Birmingham based poetry activity, to all its publishing and event-making.

Like the festival, we will strive to think about poetry in inclusive ways and embrace the multiplicity of approaches towards this glorious art.

So watch this space. Verve Poetry Press has arrived!

www.vervepoetrypress.com
@VervePoetryPres
mail@vervepoetrypress.com